Profitable Ventures: Proven Strategies to Make Money Online in 2024

Unlocking Digital Wealth

Step-by-Step Guides to Online Success

Top Trends and Methods for Maximizing Earnings

At the end of this book I will be listing some online courses that will best guid you on how to maximize your earnings in all the process covered in the book

Table of Contents

1. Introduction
2. E-Commerce and Dropshipping
   - Setting up an Online Store
   - Finding Reliable Suppliers
   - Marketing Strategies to Drive Traffic
   - Case Studies of Successful E-Commerce Businesses
3. Affiliate Marketing
   - Choosing the Right Affiliate Programs
   - Building a Niche Website or Blog
   - SEO and Content Strategies
   - Leveraging Social Media and Email Marketing
4. Freelancing and Remote Work
   - Identifying High-Demand Skills
   - Building a Strong Portfolio
   - Finding Clients on Platforms like Upwork, Fiverr, and Toptal
   - Managing and Scaling Your Freelance Business

5. Online Courses and Digital Products
   - Creating Valuable Content
   - Platforms to Sell Courses (Udemy, Teachable, etc.)
   - Marketing and Sales Strategies
   - Examples of Successful Course Creators
6. Investing in Cryptocurrencies and NFTs
   - Understanding Blockchain Technology
   - Top Cryptocurrencies to Watch in 2024
   - NFT Creation and Trading
   - Risk Management and Security Tips
7. Social Media Monetization
   - Growing an Audience on YouTube, Instagram, TikTok
   - Monetization Strategies (Ads, Sponsorships, Merchandise)
   - Engaging with Your Audience
   - Success Stories from Top Influencers
8. Passive Income Streams
   - Building and Monetizing a Blog or Website
   - Investing in Dividend Stocks and REITs
   - Creating and Selling Print-on-Demand Products
   - Setting Up Automated Sales Funnels
9. Future Trends and Emerging Opportunities
   - AI and Automation in Online Businesses
   - Virtual Reality and the Metaverse
   - Sustainable and Ethical Online Business Practices
   - Preparing for the Future of Online Entrepreneurship
10. Conclusion
    - Recap of Key Points
    - Encouragement and Motivation to Take Action
    - Resources for Further Learning and Development

Introduction

The digital landscape has evolved dramatically over the past few years, offering unprecedented opportunities for those looking to make money online. In 2024, the internet is a vast marketplace where individuals can leverage various platforms and strategies to generate income. This book will guide you through the latest and most effective methods to build a successful online business, whether you're looking to earn a side income or replace your full-time job.

E-Commerce and Dropshipping

Setting Up an Online Store:

Creating an online store has never been easier, thanks to platforms like Shopify, WooCommerce, and BigCommerce. Start by selecting a niche that interests you and has market demand. Research your target audience to understand their needs and preferences. Choose a platform that suits your technical skills and budget, then design your store with a user-friendly interface and mobile responsiveness in mind.

Finding Reliable Suppliers:

Dropshipping allows you to sell products without holding inventory. Partner with reliable suppliers through platforms like AliExpress, Oberlo, and SaleHoo. Ensure they offer quality products, reasonable prices, and timely shipping. Establish good communication to manage orders and address any issues promptly.

Marketing Strategies to Drive Traffic:

Effective marketing is crucial for driving traffic to your e-commerce store. Utilize SEO techniques to improve your store's visibility on search engines. Leverage social media platforms like Facebook, Instagram, and Pinterest to reach your target audience. Consider running paid ads and influencer partnerships to boost your store's exposure and sales.

Case Studies of Successful E-Commerce Businesses:

Explore real-life examples of entrepreneurs who have built successful e-commerce businesses. Analyze their strategies, challenges, and achievements to gain insights and inspiration for your own venture.

Affiliate Marketing

Choosing the Right Affiliate Programs:

Affiliate marketing involves promoting products or services and earning a commission for each sale made through your referral. Choose reputable affiliate programs that align with your niche and audience. Popular affiliate networks include Amazon Associates, ClickBank, and ShareASale.

SEO and Content Strategies:

Implement SEO best practices, such as keyword research, on-page optimization, and backlink building, to improve your website's ranking. Create engaging and informative content, including reviews, tutorials, and comparison articles, to encourage readers to click on your affiliate links.

Leveraging Social Media and Email Marketing:

Promote your affiliate content on social media platforms like Facebook, Twitter, and LinkedIn. Build an email list by offering valuable incentives, such as free guides or exclusive discounts. Send regular newsletters to nurture your audience and drive traffic to your affiliate offers.

Freelancing and Remote Work

Identifying High-Demand Skills:

The gig economy continues to thrive, offering numerous opportunities for freelancers and remote workers. Identify skills that are in high demand, such as web development, graphic design, digital marketing, and writing. Invest in continuous learning to stay competitive in your chosen field.

Building a Strong Portfolio:

Showcase your skills and expertise by creating a professional portfolio. Include samples of your work, client testimonials, and case studies that demonstrate your ability to deliver results. A strong portfolio will help you attract clients and secure higher-paying projects.

Finding Clients on Platforms like Upwork, Fiverr, and Toptal:

Join popular freelancing platforms where you can create a profile and bid on projects. Upwork, Fiverr, and Toptal are excellent places to start. Tailor your proposals to each client's needs, highlighting your relevant experience and how you can add value to their project.

Managing and Scaling Your Freelance Business:

Efficiently manage your time and resources to handle multiple projects. Use project management tools like Trello, Asana, and Slack to stay organized. As your business grows, consider outsourcing tasks or collaborating with other freelancers to scale your operations.

Online Courses and Digital Products

Creating Valuable Content:

Leverage your expertise by creating online courses and digital products, such as e-books, templates, and software. Identify topics that resonate with your audience and provide actionable insights or solutions. High-quality content will attract more customers and boost your reputation.

Platforms to Sell Courses (Udemy, Teachable, etc.):

Choose platforms that offer robust features and a large user base. Udemy, Teachable, and Coursera are popular options for hosting and selling online courses. These platforms provide tools for course creation, marketing, and sales management.

Marketing and Sales Strategies:

Promote your courses and digital products through your website, social media, and email marketing. Offer limited-time discounts or free trials to encourage sign-ups. Gather testimonials and reviews from satisfied customers to build credibility and attract more students.

Examples of Successful Course Creators:

Study successful online course creators to understand their strategies and techniques. Analyze their course structure, marketing efforts, and engagement methods to apply similar practices in your own business.

Investing in Cryptocurrencies and NFTs

Understanding Blockchain Technology:

Blockchain technology underpins cryptocurrencies and NFTs. It offers a decentralized, transparent, and secure way to record transactions. Familiarize yourself with blockchain basics to understand how it enables digital assets and their potential applications.

Top Cryptocurrencies to Watch in 2024:

Stay updated with the latest trends in the cryptocurrency market. Bitcoin, Ethereum, and emerging altcoins like Solana and Cardano offer investment opportunities. Research each cryptocurrency's use case, development team, and market potential before investing.

NFT Creation and Trading:

Non-fungible tokens (NFTs) represent unique digital assets. Create and sell NFTs on platforms like OpenSea, Rarible, and Foundation. Ensure your NFTs have intrinsic value, such as digital art, collectibles, or virtual real estate, to attract buyers.

Risk Management and Security Tips:

Investing in cryptocurrencies and NFTs carries risks. Diversify your portfolio, stay informed about market trends, and use secure wallets for storing your digital assets. Be cautious of scams and avoid investing more than you can afford to lose.

Social Media Monetization

Growing an Audience on YouTube, Instagram, TikTok:

Building a large and engaged audience on social media platforms can be lucrative. Focus on creating high-quality, consistent content that resonates with your target audience. Engage with your followers through comments, live streams, and collaborations with other creators.

Monetization Strategies (Ads, Sponsorships, Merchandise):

Once you have a substantial following, monetize through various channels. Enable ads on YouTube, partner with brands for sponsored content, and sell merchandise or digital products. Diversify your income streams to maximize earnings and reduce reliance on a single source.

Engaging with Your Audience:

Maintain a strong connection with your audience by responding to comments, hosting Q&A sessions, and sharing behind-the-scenes content. Building a loyal community increases your influence and opens up more monetization opportunities.

Engaging with Your Audience:

Maintain a strong connection with your audience by responding to comments, hosting Q&A sessions, and sharing behind-the-scenes content. Building a loyal community increases your influence and opens up more monetization opportunities.

Success Stories from Top Influencers:

Learn from successful social media influencers who have built profitable careers from their online presence. Analyze their strategies for content creation, audience engagement, and monetization. Understanding their journey can provide valuable insights and inspiration for your own path to social media success.

Passive Income Streams

Building and Monetizing a Blog or Website:

Creating a blog or website focused on a specific niche can generate passive income through ads, sponsored posts, and affiliate marketing. Choose a niche with consistent demand, produce high-quality content, and use SEO techniques to attract organic traffic. Platforms like WordPress and Squarespace make it easy to set up and manage your site.

Investing in Dividend Stocks and REITs:

Dividend stocks and real estate investment trusts (REITs) offer regular income with the potential for capital appreciation. Research and invest in companies with a history of stable and growing dividends. REITs allow you to invest in real estate without owning property directly, providing diversification and steady income.

Creating and Selling Print-on-Demand Products:

Print-on-demand (POD) allows you to sell custom-designed products without holding inventory. Use platforms like Printful, Teespring, and Redbubble to create and sell items such as t-shirts, mugs, and phone cases. Focus on creating unique, appealing designs that resonate with your target audience.

Setting Up Automated Sales Funnels:

Automated sales funnels can generate passive income by guiding potential customers through the buying process. Use tools like ClickFunnels and Leadpages to create landing pages, email sequences, and upsell offers. Automating these processes ensures consistent revenue with minimal ongoing effort.

Future Trends and Emerging Opportunities

AI and Automation in Online Businesses:

Artificial intelligence (AI) and automation are transforming online businesses by increasing efficiency and reducing costs. Implement AI-powered tools for customer service, marketing, and data analysis to stay competitive. Keep an eye on emerging technologies that can offer new business opportunities.

Virtual Reality and the Metaverse:

Virtual reality (VR) and the metaverse are creating new ways to interact and do business online. Explore opportunities in VR content creation, virtual real estate, and metaverse-based services. Early adoption of these technologies can position you ahead of the curve in an evolving market.

Sustainable and Ethical Online Business Practices:

Consumers are increasingly valuing sustainability and ethics in business. Incorporate eco-friendly practices and transparent operations into your online ventures. Highlight your commitment to sustainability in your marketing to attract conscious consumers and build a positive brand image.

Preparing for the Future of Online Entrepreneurship:

Stay informed about the latest trends and technological advancements to adapt your business strategies. Invest in continuous learning and skill development to remain agile and innovative. Network with other entrepreneurs and industry experts to share knowledge and explore new opportunities.

Conclusion

In this book, we've explored a variety of proven strategies to make money online in 2024. From e-commerce and dropshipping to affiliate marketing, freelancing, online courses, and investing in cryptocurrencies, each method offers unique opportunities and challenges. Social media monetization and passive income streams provide additional avenues for generating revenue.

The key to success in online entrepreneurship is taking consistent action. Start small, set achievable goals, and build on your successes. Embrace failures as learning experiences and stay persistent in your efforts. With dedication and the right strategies, you can achieve financial freedom and build a thriving online business.

To continue your journey, explore the following resources:
- Online courses on platforms like Coursera, Udemy, and LinkedIn Learning
- Books on entrepreneurship and digital marketing
- Blogs and podcasts by industry experts
- Online communities and forums for networking and support

Additional Resources

Books:
- "The Lean Startup" by Eric Ries
- "Crushing It!" by Gary Vaynerchuk
- "Dotcom Secrets" by Russell Brunson

Websites:
- Entrepreneur.com
- NeilPatel.com
- SmartPassiveIncome.com

Tools:
- Google Analytics (for tracking website traffic)
- Canva (for graphic design)
- Buffer (for social media management)

Best online courses to check out

1. Crypto profit kit

2. Lucrative Ecommerce Business Blueprint (LEBB)

3. Digital Marketing For Beginners: DMB

4. Affiliate Income Pilot Blueprint (AIP Blueprint)

5. VIDEO CONTENT WORKSHOP

Thank you for taking the time to read "Profitable Ventures: Proven Strategies to Make Money Online in 2024". I hope you found the information valuable and that it helps you on your journey to online success.

Your feedback is incredibly important to me and to future readers. If you enjoyed the book and found it useful, please consider leaving a positive review on Amazon. Your review will help others discover this book and benefit from its insights.

Thank you once again for your support. Wishing you all the best on your journey to success!

Sincerely,

Borngreat mmesomachukwu onwe

www.ingramcontent.com/pod-product-compliance
Lightning Source LLC
Chambersburg PA
CBHW072055230526
45479CB00010B/1089